A Smile Gives You Shivers, Still

Lynne G. Schwalbe

PublishAmerica
Baltimore

First printing

At the specific preference of the author, PublishAmerica allowed this work to remain exactly as the author intended, verbatim, without editorial input.

Chapter 1: MUSART, Los Angeles, California, 1939 (no longer in existence)
Chapter 2 : Michael Ray Creative Photography, Glendale, California (no longer in existence)
Chapter 3 : Richard Williams, Richard Williams Photography, Glendale, California, who is still in business.
The photograph of the back cover photograph is unknown, but it was taken in 1996.

ISBN: 1-4137-9819-5
PUBLISHED BY PUBLISHAMERICA, LLLP
www.publishamerica.com
Baltimore

Printed in the United States of America

Acknowledgments

The poem "Clutter" was published in *Poetic Voices* (www.poeticvoices.com), March 2004

The poems, "I Wonder", "Our Miracle" and "Turnabout" were published in *Verdugo Verses 2005*, Anthology of John Steven McGroarty Chapter of California Federation of Chaparral Poets, Inc., April 2005. The website of California Federation of Chaparral Poets, Inc., can be found at www.chaparralpoets.org.

Credits

The photograph for Chapter 1 was created by MUSART, Los Angeles, California, in 1939 (no longer in existence).

The photograph for Chapter 2 was created by Michael Ray Creative Photography, Glendale, CA, in 1974 (no longer in existence).

The photograph for Chapter 3 was created by Richard Williams Photography, Glendale, CA, in 1986. Permission for use was granted by Richard Williams, March 18, 2005.

The photograph on the back cover was taken in 1996; photographer unknown.

The manuscript prepared for the publisher was typed by Ursula T. Gibson, using Microsoft Word *Times New Roman* 12 pt. and 10 pt.

Dedication

To our darling daughter, Lori Kilgore.

To our special son, George Schwalbe.

To our grandchildren, Lisa Nicole and Gerald Anthony,

and our great-granddaughter, Melina Marie:

The Joys of our Lives.

A special thank-you to Ursula T. Gibson,
my mentor and friend,
who awakened my Muse after a long slumber.

Lynne G. Schwalbe
2005

Biography

I learned poetry from my father, Jack Greenhill (also known as Jack Greenberg), who was a published poet.

I was born in 1936 in Glendale, California, to Mollie and Jack Greenhill. I grew up in Los Angeles and graduated from Fairfax High School in 1953.

I married Max Schwalbe in 1954, after completing one year of college. Our family includes our daughter, Lori Elizabeth, and her husband, Jerry Kilgore; our son George Craig Schwalbe; two grandchildren, Gerald Anthony Kilgore and Lisa Nicole Kilgore; three grown granddaughters, and their husbands, Nikki Kilgore and Ron Arciaga, Kristy Rodriguez and Cheo Rodriguez, and Gina Graham and Steve Graham; and our great-granddaughter, Melina Marie Rodriguez.

Max and I separated in 1996, and reconciled in 2001. We live in Burbank, California. I am a retired full-charge bookkeeper.

I hope my experience and poetry will touch your heart.

Lynne G. Schwalbe

A Smile Gives You Shivers, Still

A Smile Gives You Shivers, Still

1

The Early Years

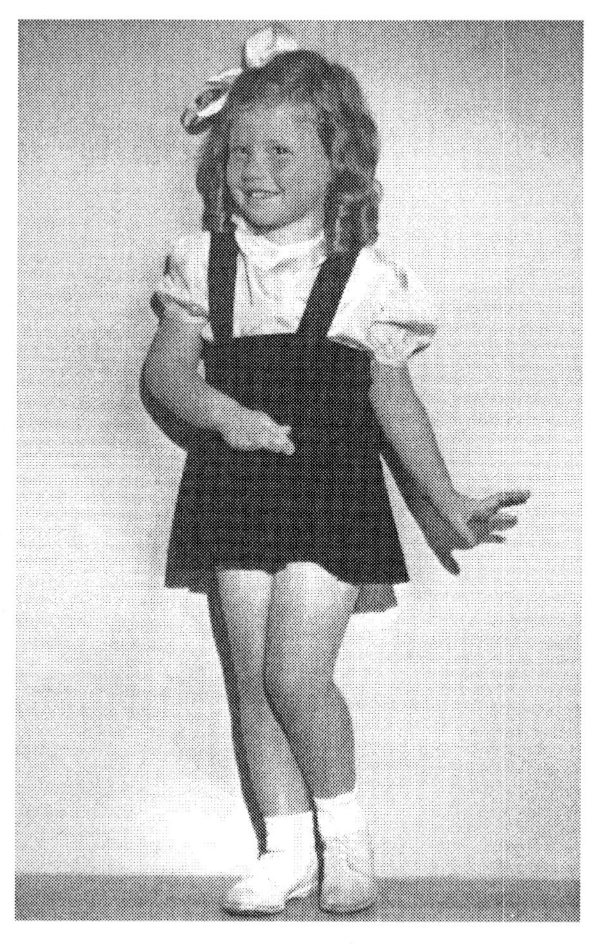

The photograph for Chapter I was created by Musart, Los Angeles, CA, in 1939

Mollie

A three-pound premie
She had a rocky start.
Rheumatic fever
Then weakened her heart.

In spite of frail health
She was an optimist.
Her cheery disposition
No one could resist.

Bright ray of sunshine,
Such beauty and grace!
With sweet, lilting voice
And smile on her face.

The perfect Mother
She gladdened my heart.
Then Death came calling
And tore us apart.

"Your Life was Warmth and Cheer
Who knew you loved you, Dear."

(This poem won 2nd Place in the McGroarty Chapter, California
Federation of Chaparral Poets, Inc., Monthly Contest, 2-26-05.)

Jack

Oppressed in Russia, they fled to the U.S.A.
My dad always said he was born on the high sea.
Ship manifest stated he was twelve when he came,
So his early life will remain a mystery.

His first job in New York when he was only twelve—
By bicycle, singing telegrams were quickly brought.
Third grade and law school, his only formal training.
The rest of his extensive learning was self-taught.

Farmer, insurance man, auto racer, and more,
Actor, poet, attorney for fifty-two years.
Dad had two grown children when he married my mom;
Traveled life's road together through laughter and tears.

He had a gruff nature, but was quite gentle, too.
Patient, he taught me to love music and poetry,
Treated me as an equal, always with respect.
With him for my Dad, I was lucky as could be!

"Of gentle heart and mighty deed,
Truth and Justice were your creed."

Mom and Dad

Dad went to Long Beach to watch the ships come in;
Saw a lovely lady on a deck far above.
He rushed up to meet her, fell instantly in love.
From this chance meeting, their new life would begin.

A thousand poems in twenty-six years—token
Of his great love for his beautiful young bride.
Adoringly shared good and bad side by side;
Throughout their marriage, not a harsh word spoken.

Far too soon, Death came and stole his love away.
He missed and cherished her to his dying day.

The Moon

(First poem, age 5 years.)

When I was young
I thought the Moon
Was a fingernail
Thrown into the Sky

But now I know
It is only the MOON.

Oops!

A beautiful baby girl was born
But the bureaucrats blew it, by golly!
Ignorance is bliss, and the years flew by
Until the boner was found by Mollie.

In '50 fortune frowned fleetingly
On this close-knit, fun-loving family.
To travel to foreign lands was the plan
Stopped by the flummoxed bureaucracy.

The birth certificate was clearly wrong.
It claimed the premie girl incorrectly
As a full-term boy, so the callous clerk
Said, "Come, bring the child. Prove the sex to me!"

We can't help but wonder why this occurred.
Was Windsor Hospital so busy that night?
What happened to the boy called a girl?
We wondered, was he aware of his plight?

Harried and hassled, with child in hand
Mom hurried to City Hall to right this wrong.
Happy at last! Her Honey-Girl is shown
Just as she should have been all along.

Conspiracy

I hated those auburn finger curls
Cascading down almost to my waist!
Nine, I wanted to be rid of them,
But Mom felt I was acting in haste.

Each night she carefully rolled my hair
In dreaded white strips of cloth, just so
Every morning she could shape each curl.
Then to school I'd reluctantly go.

Mom's source of joy was my agony.
Girls played with my curls, the boys did worse!
They dipped my tresses in the ink-well
As I tried to study. What a curse!

My pleas for shorter hair were ignored.
Desperate, I did not know what to do.
That summer my New Jersey cousins
So mercifully came to my rescue!

Charles, Lindy and I were quite bored.
'Twas another hot and muggy day.
Sent to the sunporch, what could we do?
I suggested a new game to play.

"Let's play barbershop!" I exclaimed.
'Twas a great idea, we did agree.
Charles gathered towel, stool, scissors,
And I sat there waiting eagerly.

"Which curl should I cut? How short should it be?"
"The one in the back," I said gleefully.
Quickly Charley had a long curl in hand,
And I knew at last I would be free!

He danced with his prize; we shouted praise.
Soon Mom and Aunt Flo heard the noise.
Mom was distraught when she saw the result;
Aunt Flo laughed and said, "Boys will be boys!"

Naughty, what would my punishment be?
To my great surprise, I was not blamed.
"Charles is the oldest; it's his fault."
By his mother, poor Charley was framed!

Mom calmed down. An appointment was made.
To the elegant salon went we.
I had a beautiful short hairdo!
I was happy as I could be!

(This poem won 4th Place for 2004, and 1st Place on 4-24-04 in
the McGroarty Chapter, California Federation of Chaparral Poets,
Inc. Monthly Contest.)

Betsy Lou

Better take those inflamed tonsils out, right away!
Exclaimed the doctor so very seriously.
The verdict was the same for Ethel. (We were five.)
So, together we had the dreaded surgery.
You will get a surprise," Mom said. "Just wait and see!"

Lucky Ethel! Her new doll had baby-soft skin.
Oh, I envied her! A porcelain doll, mine since age one;
Unique hand-made clothes from head to toe to begin;

Mom's beautiful auburn curls set her face aglow.
Yes, Betsy Lou was gorgeous; I was too young to know.

Finally, as I grew older, I loved her dearly.
Inseparable companions for so many years.
Remembering how special she was brings me pleasure.
She shared all my secrets, my laughter, and my tears.
Then she was packed away, one day to reappear.

Delighted to have a daughter to give her to;
Oh, the fun I had getting Betsy Lou ready!
Lori loved her as much as I did. Now she waits.
Lisa will have a daughter one day, hopefully!

Turnabout

Turnabout Theatre on La Cienega street—
Unquestionably my favorite childhood treat!
Remember the trolley seats with names to charm you?
Now 'n' Then, Tweedledum 'n' Tweedledee, Tried 'n' True,
Adam 'n' Eve, Hollywood 'n' Vine, to name a few!
Best of all was the entertainment awaiting you.
Oh, I loved the puppets! With "Haydn Trio" we were blessed.
Ultimate pleasure! Turnabout for Act Two, I'd suggest —
To enjoy comedy, opera, drama at its best.

To this day I recall "Disgruntled." Thanks, Lotte Goslar!
Harry Burnett's "Glow Worm" made him a star!
Elsa Lanchester was a treasure, the divinest!
Antics delighted us, and her acting thrilled each guest.
Turnabout Theatre! That place always made me happy.
Relaxation, laughter, fun, and comradery;
Entertainment at its finest, etched in my memory.

To "E" or Not to "E"

Dad had two authors he greatly admired,
And he gave their names to the son he sired.
My brother was teased and taunted as a lad
For "Byron Voltaire" was his name, thanks to Dad!

When I was expected, Byron did decree
That it was his great desire to name me.
"Lynne" is my first name, and that suits me just fine,
But with "Eda," Byron said, "Vengeance is mine!"

The furor over my name did not subside.
Some used the "E" to end "Lynne", some let it slide.
Birth certificate says "L-Y-N-N-E".
Soon Mom left the "E" off intentionally.

My scrapbook is proof beyond any doubt.
"E" was a letter I couldn't do without.
At twelve, with no fuss or ceremony
I again spelled my name "L-Y-N-N-E".

"Lynne" means "a small pool" or "ruddy complected".
A nicer-meaning name I'd have selected!
"Eda" comes from Hebrew. It means, "renewer";
No wonder I'm not a watcher, but a doer!

Mom and Dad knew "Eda" was a name I hated.
So its constant use they most kindly abated.
Whenever I was scolded, they punished me
Calling, "LYNNE-EDA, come immediately!"

Because one Lynne Greenhill was not quite enough,
Fairfax High had two, so my school days were rough.
My parents were called in day after day
And told I was failing, but I got the "A!"

When I married, "Eda" was dropped permanently.
With maiden name initial, I'm "Schwalbe, Lynne G."
When our children were born, we chose carefully,
Giving them names we liked, and we hope they agree!

First Love

He was tall, dark and handsome.
We were youngsters when we met.
"Lee" was my first love's name.
His sweet smile, I'll ne'er forget.

B'nai Brith and A.Z.A.
Had a dance one summer night.
Mom asked, "Why don't you go, Dear?"
Naught to do, I said, "All right."

The boys stood against one wall,
The girls were across the way.
He came over and said, "Hi!"
It was a red-letter day!

We danced, talked, had lemonade.
He walked me home just past ten.
My heart was all a-flutter!
He said, "Let's meet soon again!"

I was thirteen, he sixteen.
Would the age difference annoy?
Would our parents object? Oh, no!
He was a "nice Jewish boy"!

Inseparable from the first,
Our love was hard to ignore.
Picnics, movies, dances shared;
A hug, kiss, dared not do more!

I was ready to start Fairfax High,
Lee took me under his wing.
A Senior now, he knew it all.
High school became exciting!

We were happy for three years.
I thought it would never end.
Overnight, he disappeared!
Why, I could not comprehend.

His parents were quite upset.
Thought our romance would not do.
They had lofty goals for him
And sent him to N.Y.U.!

Sent away so suddenly!
My friends helped discover why.
I was not "religious enough";
He was to be a Rabbi!

It was so hard to accept
Our romance ended this way.
My first love has a special
Place in my heart to this day!

In 1997 I saw
His last name on the obit page.
Could it be his family?
We're getting close to that age.

I wrote a card. Lee answered!
"Got your note. Aunt Sarah died.
Love to hear from you! Please call."
Of course, I promptly replied.

We talked for half an hour.
"I remember dating you.
You were my first love," he said.
I replied, "You were mine, too!"

We exchanged our histories.
He did what he desired.
He sang on the Broadway stage;
Was Rabbi, now retired.

Sells real estate in Tucson
He's been wed 42 years.
He has two sons, one daughter.
They give him joy and some tears.

Three grandkids keep him busy
In his retirement years.
"Call if you're coming this way.
I would love to see you, Dear."

What happened to your first love?
You don't often get to know.
Eight years since we reconnected,
See him? I'd love to go!

Blind Date

My father fixed me up on a blind date one day.
I was a mere sixteen, the man was thirty-three!
I cried. Then I pleaded, "Please, please don't make me go!"
Dad replied, "My word is my bond, my guarantee!"

The dreaded day arrived, so I prepared to go.
Came Eastern Indian in white turban and silk coat.
"I'll take good care of your precious little flower.
We'll be home before ten." I could just see him gloat!

Entering his car, I did not know what to expect.
The drive-in "Bronco Busters", our destination.
Soon his romantic intentions were very clear.
He moved close to me with determination.

As he came closer, I slid across the front seat.
So, quickly he followed and tried to embrace me.
Pressed against the door, I frantically opened it,
Ran around and sat behind the steering wheel, free!

Unfortunately, my freedom didn't last long.
He reversed directions, came close to me once more.
I opened the door, ran around the car again
And ended up exactly where I was before.

He was so persistent! "Your heart is made of ice!"
I protested, "Take me home immediately!"
Reluctantly he did as I commanded him.
Told Dad, "Thank you for sharing your jewel with me."

Mom and Dad were relieved to know I was okay.
Dad said he'd not arrange another date for me.
And I was thrilled to be home again, safe and sound.
A good end to a bad adventure, we did agree!

Gumdrop Hill

(A Bedtime Story for Lori and George)

This is the story of a magic place.
It's called the Land of the Gumdrop Hill.
It was told to me when I was quite small.
If I close my eyes, I can see it still.

I was about your age the first time I took
The long journey to this land of sweets.
It's a lovely place for all boys and girls,
With all kinds of delicious treats.

Come traveling with me, and we shall see
The many wonders of this magic land.
Get on my lap, and we'll be on our way.
Here we go! Isn't this simply grand?

We're almost there. See the Lemonade Lake
With ice cube ducklings swimming around?
And look! Over there! A popsicle tree
With its flavors dripping to the ground.

At last, there amid some marshmallow clouds
Stands the Gumdrop Hill to welcome you.
Scamper along to have some fun and treats;
Go eat your fill until you are through.

Drink from Raspberry River to end your thirst,
Then let's run to the Gingerbread House.
Hurry down winding Licorice Lane;
You might meet and eat a chocolate mouse!

Sample the fluffy white marshmallow clouds;
Taste everything in sight before you stop.
But don't eat too much, or your tummy will ache,
And you'll think for sure that you will POP!

As you nap, elves water the Popsicle tree,
And fill the Lemonade Lake to the brim.
They fix Gingerbread Houses and fences, too,
And the chocolate mouse, can't forget him!

Soon everything is in order again,
And there's only one thing left to do.
The elves will whisper something in your ear.
I know what they'll tell you, do you?

"Remember the goodies of Gumdrop Hill
Are special treats for those who are good;
Who eat all their food, watch their manners, too,
And who mind their parents as they should."

"We know to be greedy is certainly wrong.
To share with others is what we should do.
Take some for yourself and leave the rest
For the children who will follow you."

So many times before I grew up
I went to the Land of Gumdrop Hill.
I love those goodies and friendly elves.
If I close my eyes, I can see it still.

1954

Our wedding day was planned for June twenty-seventh.
Then I was crowned Queen on the "Queen for a Day" show!
"Honeymoon starts June seventeenth. Will you be wed?"
I answered Jack Bailey, "We'll be ready to go!"

Rabbi came to the house, signed the certificate.
Judge Mosk told Mom, "They're married, though no vows were said."
"There goes my baby, and she isn't even married!"
Cried Mom as we boarded the plane. Was my face red!

Lost!

Lost! Our little son was only three.
Where could our adventuresome lad be?
"George! Where are you?" was our fervent plea.
Here one moment, then gone instantly!

Our sweet little boy had flown the nest.
All our neighbors soon joined in the quest.
Desperate, we called North Hollywood's finest.
For two hours the police did their best.

We looked in every room carefully.
Then the yard endured our scrutiny.
Sirens blared, oh, so very loudly.
Four or five squad cars searched futilely.

I was crying uncontrollably.
Daddy and Grandpa searched endlessly.
Lori feared her brother lost permanently.
Where could our adventuresome son be?

We searched the house again, exhausted.
Closets, toy chests, every step retread.
We feared the worst. Thankfully, instead,
There he was! Asleep under his bed!

Halloween, 1965

Second-grader Lori needed a costume for the parade,
So, of course, pre-school George had to have an outfit, too.
Sick in bed for weeks with Mono, I didn't know what to do,
So I called their Grandpa Jack, who quickly came to our aid.

Shopping was not Dad's forte, so store costumes just would not do.
"Would you like to be a Princess, Lori? Or blushing bride?"
"Do you want to be Batman, George?" They simply could not decide.
It was clear it would be Grandpa's choice. "I'll just surprise you!"

Dad was great at making things. His workshop was legendary.
So he checked each nook and cranny to see what he could use.
"These costumes must be original, fun, and sure to amuse."
He found what he needed. The unknown was temporary!

Dad painted the box white; then he cut three holes. He did this twice.
Soon black dots of different numbers were painted on each side.
Excited, the children slipped on their costumes, beaming with pride.
In a mere instant, Lori and George were a pair of dice!

Lori wore her costume to school, and compliments came her way.
At noon I brought George to school to watch the festivities.
The teacher saw him in the audience. "Join your sister, please!"
Halloween was a great success! A very special day!

The Ring Cycle

To profess his love to his beloved Mollie,
Very special his proposal would have to be.
So Dad designed the engagement ring joyfully
And had it made by Tiffany's in 1933.

The old mine-cut diamond nestled comfortably
In the woven golden basket for all to see,
While platinum swans held the handles in their beaks.
Of love for Mollie, the ring eloquently speaks!

Mother wore this masterpiece with love and pride.
She was excited and happy to be Jack's bride!
For twenty-seven years, they did all side by side;
Soon, far too soon, his darling, his young love, died.

Dad kept the ring for eight long years, and then did declare
I was mature enough to be trusted with its care.
First night I left it on my dresser carelessly.
Lost in the fire, why I left it there still haunts me.

Three dreadful days in the cold January rain,
We sifted through the rubble again and again.
With window screening we sifted through the debris,
Just to satisfy demands of the insurance company!

We had Dad's original drawings, fortunately,
So the ring could be recreated perfectly.
On Mother's long, slender hand, it turned constantly—
On my fat finger, it stayed in place easily.

Heavy as a brick, it was wide and hard to wear.
I could not forget for a moment it was there.
To honor my Dad, I wore it as he designed;
And later had it reset with my tastes in mind.

The large diamond sat atop a high, lacy mound
With twenty-four small diamonds scattered all around.
It was quite lovely, but it was very plain to see
That this huge piece of jewelry was not right for me.

So I had the large center sparkler reset once more.
With Mom's wedding ring stones, it's a treasure I adore.
And the several small diamonds were used creatively
To adorn a Star of David for our dear Lori.

At a New Year's Eve party, several years ago
A psychic entertained us at the midnight show.
He asked for an object; my ring was offered, so
By touch he told about Mom, what he could not know.

Wearing this ring brings many happy memories.
I feel Mom and Dad especially close to me.
An heirloom! A tradition! It will always be
Handed down to each generation, lovingly.

Dad's Advice

Never go to bed angry with your husband or wife.
Examine, end differences before you sleep.
Victims of arguments and marital strife
End all chance to know contentment, wedded bliss,
Romance, love, and a long harmonious life.

Guide your children to love and to compromise.
Offering them knowledge by example is wise.

To grow up in a home filled with love and joy
Ought to be the right of every girl and boy.

But know that this goal is not an easy task.
Easier said than done, effort is a must.
Doing our very best is all we can ask.

Anger corrodes the soul and rots the heart.
Nothing's harder to break than a bad habit, so
Give love, patience, understanding from the start.
Remember that what you give is what you get.
Yes, rewards are many! Just follow your heart.

(This poem won 3rd Place on 7-24-04 in the McGroarty Chapter,
California Federation of Chaparral Poets, Inc., Monthly Contest.)

11

Through the Years

This photograph was created by Michael Ray Creative
Photography, Glendale, CA in 1974.
Michael Ray Creative Photography is no longer in existence.

Passover

(A Charlet sequence; syllabic, 6, 6, 9, 2)

Passover! Time of joy!
Freedom from Pharaoh's grasp!
Family and friends around the table;
Seder!

Matzoh: flat bread of haste.
Bitter herbs: slavery.
Roasted shankbone: Lord saved our first-born!
Seder!

Egg: Passover offering.
Charosis: bricks, mortar.
Parsley: Our thanks for Earth's rich bounty.
Seder!

The Four Questions; Ten Plagues;
The Cup of Elijah;
Passover tradition, hopes for Peace.
Seder!

Thanksgiving

Tiny tot, I remember Mom preparing the feast for days.
Happily she sang. Glorious smells! Hunger we could not deny!
Anxious to stuff ourselves full of turkey, stuffing, yams, cranberries,
New baby peas, onions, mashed potatoes and home-made pumpkin pie.
Knowing servicemen were lonely, Mom called the U.S.O. They came.
Sister, brother, cousins, their families, crowded around the table.
Grand memories of family, friends, laughter, and joy remain.
I hosted, when younger. Tradition! Did the best I was able.
Very soon, Lori was grown, with a family. It was her turn.
Invitingly, capably, the Kilgores now host the holiday.
Nothing makes us happier than to be with our family.
Grateful, we give thanks. Good times to be shared
    for many years, we pray.

Chanukah

(Tanka)

Chanukah lights!
Burn bright for eight nights!
Macabees fought.
Their freedom they sought.
Their victory, tolerance taught.

Chanukah lights!
Burn bright for eight nights!
Dreidels spin.
Gold coins we will win.
Latkes! Singing! Now, let's begin!

Happy New Year!

(Charlet Sequence)

Young, we wish years to pass;
When older, they fly by.
"Youth is wasted on the young", but why?
That's life!

The New Year has begun.
Resolutions abide!
With good health, and your love by your side,
Great Joy!

Perpetual Motion

Forty-nine years ago, as a blushing bride,
I knew my job list would be diversified.
Career, home, family kept me occupied;
And for the most part, I was quite satisfied.

Just one recurring problem made me cry.
Dishes in the sink were always piled high.
All by themselves, they seemed to multiply!
Constantly, it was time to wash and dry.

Forty-nine years five hundred eighty-eight months become.
Two thousand, five hundred forty-eight weeks of washing boredom!
That's seventeen thousand, eight hundred ninety days, and then some;
Fifty-three thousand, six hundred ninety meals, and more to come!

To be accurate and completely fair,
I really must remember to declare
Vacations and meals out ease the nightmare
And contribute greatly to my welfare!

A dishwasher was installed in nineteen sixty-nine.
At long last, freedom from dishwashing was mine!
"Pots and pans just don't get clean," Max did soon whine.
My dishwashing ways I had to redesign.

Dishes go in the washer without delay.
Pots and pans will be washed later in the day.
After dinner, most nights, all is put away.
Clean and shiny I wish my kitchen would stay!

Court & Sport

Since Max came back home in 2001, changes abound.
Some are to my liking, and some drive me crazy, I've found!
By myself I was lonely, so the companionship is grand.
But Max's obsession with Court and Sport, I can't understand!

For breakfast the television is tuned to the first Judge show.
How someone can like this noisy upheaval, I just don't know!
"He won't pay me back!" "It was a gift," is the usual claim.
I'm amazed at how low people stoop for their moment of fame!

Judge shows fill the airways for argumentative hours each day—
Litigants shout. Before you know it, the Judge joins the fray.
At ten there's two-hour respite, then the court shows are back.
Again the defendants and plaintiffs mercilessly attack.

Soon it's lunch time and another court show loudly fills the air.
I come to the table quite hungry, but full of despair.
Conversation would be lovely, peace and quiet would be bliss—
But hard as I try to explain, Max doesn't understand this!

It is evening. Court shows are gone, but sports are customary.
So, far too often, my bedroom becomes my sanctuary.
With so many Cable sports channels, the choice is endless;
Football, baseball, hockey, basketball, all add to my distress.

Jeopardy, Wheel of Fortune for dinner, and when I recline,
Then from 8:00 p.m. to 9:00 p.m., the choice is all mine.
Court & Sport are his loves, quiz and home shows are mine, so it's wise
For us to respect each other, and start to compromise!

Then and Now

"Thirty-three hundred for a car? That's Highway Robbery!
I paid eight hundred for my first— a snazzy Model T!"
"Seventeen thousand for a house, when it's not even new?
"I paid just nine thousand to build my dream house; why can't you?"
Whatever we bought, Dad told us he got his for much less;
But the difference in our salaries, he did not address.
At twenty, he worked six days per week, twelve hours each day.
The huge sum of ten dollars was his entire week's pay!
In '54, I earned a dollar an hour. That was grand!
Economics was something Dad just did not understand.
Even though prices keep going up, this fact does apply:
It takes fewer hours now to pay for the things we buy.

Remembering the talks Dad and I had, I thought for sure
I'd know much better, but my assumption was premature.
My granddaughter Lisa and I were chatting recently
About the many things we bought during our shopping spree.
"Seventy five for jeans and top? Prices never cease to amaze!"
She answered sweetly, "But Grandma, that's what things cost
these days!"
Soon we were comparing costs and wages, now and back then.
She said she wished things could be so reasonable again.
"Food for two: seven a week; mortgage a hundred or less—
Sears diamond ring, thirty bucks. Is today's way really progress?"
I quickly realized I sounded like Dad— no exaggeration!
We've come full circle, from generation to generation!

Why?

Writing on demand is quite tough.
I wait for the ideas to flow.
Inspiration lacks. I say, "Enough!"
Off to do other things, I go.

But there's one thing I know for sure.
Hop in the tub, relax in it;
That's always my writers' block cure.
Ideas come a mile a minute!

Poetry
(Cinquain)

Tanka,

Charlet, Cinquain,

Haiku, Senryu, Prose;

I'll try them all, then back to rhyme.

COMFORT!

A Wish Come True

The alarm comes on to jolt me awake.
Another hour of sleep I'd like to take!
But duty calls me for my garden's sake.
    Why must I get up at the crack of dawn?

The old sprinklers don't do the job at all.
Brown spots stay, summer, winter, spring and fall.
Bushes, trees, and the flowers seem to call.
    It's time once again to water the lawn.

For so many years, it's a constant demand.
With hat, sunglasses, and my cane in hand
I follow this most distasteful command.
    That's why I get up at the crack of dawn!

After watering, I go back to my bed.
I have so many things to do instead,
But my arthritis is agitated.
    I can't continue to water the lawn!

So I saved and I saved to end my plight.
Sprinklers were installed, to my great delight!
In just a month, the lawn is green and bright.
    No more arising at the crack of dawn!

Water glistens on each tall blade of grass
Just like miniature jewels of sparkling glass.
Mushrooms sprout, and flowers smile en masse.
    No more standing there to water the lawn!

Clutter

The piles of paper on my desk
Keep growing, no matter how I try.
They could in fact, I am quite sure,
Teach rabbits how to multiply!

They're neatly stored in several stacks
According to their urgency.
Day after day, they are ignored,
Usurped by some emergency.

The papers seem to taunt and tease:
"Where were you, Madam, yesterday?
You promised to take care of us.
Alas, again you've gone astray."

Determined, I work at my desk
When clutter gets the best of me.
Some things are shuffled, put aside;
Some are completed easily.

Just when I think I'm all caught up
The mailman makes a delivery.
Soon the mess is worse than ever—
It must be a conspiracy!

(This poem was selected as first place poem in the California
Federation of Chaparral Poets, Inc., McGroarty Chapter, Monthly
Contest, Jan. 2004.)

My Collection

(Sonnet)

They can't be hidden in my drawer.
They can't be purchased in a store.
They can't be found in bag or box.
They can't be snuggled with my sox.

They come in all colors and sizes.
They come planned or as surprises.
They came to me, a child at play.
They come to me along life's way.

Some I'd like to change or forget.
Some I cherish, some I regret.
Some goad me and often annoy.
Some give me comfort and great joy.

They are my companions, and they please.
They are my precious memories.

Autumn

Delicate leaves shiver in the breeze
Holding onto the branches for dear life.
They turn from green to gold to brown as days pass.
Finally letting go,
They float to the ground gracefully,
Covering the lawn with a blanket of many colors.

He Is Lost!

He stops and sniffs the grass,
Runs back and forth frantically.
I go outside and call him.
He comes immediately.

I pet his soft brown head;
Tickle his ears, and talk gently.
Look for a tag, but find none.
Who could his careless owners be?

He licks my hands and face.
I want to keep him, this I know.
Someone must be missing him.
Perhaps a child cries, and so

Sadly, I place the ad.
"Lost. Sweet pup. Identify."
There were no calls! He's mine at last!
We won't have to say, "Goodbye."

Today Is Sunday

Today is Sunday, the "day of rest."
From my schedule, you'd never have guessed!
Fixing breakfast starts my busy day.
Then it's six loads of wash underway.

Light wash, dark wash, sheets, towels and more—
The piles adorn my kitchen floor.
Stains treated, the first load is started.
Wash, dry, fold. Dirt and laundry parted!

So many things need my attention.
Full baskets, unmade beds must be done.
Desk work and projects are calling me,
But I'd like to sit and watch T.V.!

Reading the *Times* is a day-long chore—
News, comics, magazines, and much more.
Letter writing I'd like to ignore—
Getting them is fun; answering a bore!

It's time for dinner and the dishes.
Day is done, and these are my wishes.
A maid would be nice, a robot, O.K.
I declare next Sunday a Holiday!

Haiku Medley

Icy, bitter cold
The wind howls all through the night.
Now trees stand naked.

Loudly the rain falls.
Endless shards of sparkling glass
Nourishing the Earth.

The rain stops at last!
Arc of many colors thrills.
Glorious rainbow!

The sun shines brightly
Warming the Earth. Flowers sprout.
Children laugh and play.

Stars fill the night sky.
Nature's electricity
Disappears at dawn.

(This poem won 1st prize 4-30-05 in the McGroarty Chapter,
California Federation of Chaparral Poets, Inc., Monthly Contest)

Persistence

There's a thin me inside trying to get out,
But she's been hiding so long she's hard to find.
I know I must lose weight; my health is at stake.
I must change my ways. Now to make up my mind!

Clothes in my closet from small to extra large;
My joints cause pain, I walk with difficulty.
Jobs take me longer so I procrastinate.
With the extra pounds, energy eludes me.

Dieting is hard, counting calories a chore.
Temptation calls. Feeling deprived is no fun.
But the New Year brings hope, so I'll try again.
Determined, the battle of the bulge will be won!

Credo

(Senryu)

The past: Cherish it!

The present: Live life gladly!

The future: Dream dreams.

New Kitty

So quietly she walks on her pink padded paws.
In an instant, she attacks with tiny, sharp claws.
One moment she sleeps on my lap, motor running;
Then pounces on her toy mouse with speed and cunning.
The scratching post ignored, no furniture is spared.
With sandpaper-tongue kisses, her love is declared.
She's independent, and it's very plain to see
This fluffy ball of fur rules our home completely!

The Stranger

A tall, dark stranger stands across the walkway.
Solemn, dressed in black, he keeps staring at me.
I can't escape his gaze; he won't go away.
I'm absolutely terrified! Who is he?

Can he be just an innocent traveler
Enjoying the sights this lovely winter day?
Or is he a darker soul— the Grim Reaper,
Waiting for his next victim to come this way?

Dear God! Let it not be me he's waiting for!
I'm not ready to go! I've so much to do —
My family to love, and the world to explore;
Goals to accomplish before my days are through!

I turn and run, but there is no place to go.
I'm scared, but I'm filled with curiosity.
I look. He's gone! Who he was, I'll never know.
But I'm still here! He wasn't waiting for me!

Dear Ursula,

You have taught me to appreciate

   poetry that does not rhyme,

And to cherish

   poetry that does.

You have taught me poetic forms

   I did not know,

And have enriched my writing

   because of them.

You have shown me

    the enjoyment of writing,

And introduced me to

    the discipline I need to write.

You have expanded my world

    with knowledge.

Best of all,

    you have become my friend.

    Love,

    Lynne Schwalbe

My Birthday, 2004

(Shakespearean Sonnet)

Today's the anniversary of my birth.
In the blink of an eye, I'm suddenly sixty-eight.
Here's some advice. Take it for what it's worth.
Enjoy each day. Live before it's too late.

Continue to learn something amazing each day.
Do what you can to help all humankind.
Be passionate about your work and play.
Love one another, and love you will find.

Cherish your family and friends above all.
Some money is fine, but do not chase wealth.
Delight in the Earth's beauties, large and small.
You're lucky as long as you have your health.

No one can convince me that I am old!
Life's sweet treasures are a joy to behold!

Unanswered

Which came first, the music or the words?
Which came first, the chicken or the egg?
What's more important, the song or the birds?
What's more important, the arm or the leg?

Examples abound, need another?
We can ponder deeply every one.
Life's not complete, one without the other;
It doesn't matter when all's said and done.

The Old Lady

My Dodge Aries has turned eighteen.
She is not aging gracefully.
So many things need to be fixed,
But they're all past the guarantee!

Her signal lights have stopped working
So they must be repaired today.
Her door locks are temperamental.
I wonder what I'll have to pay.

Her bald tires need replacing.
Her clock refuses to tell time.
Gauge broken, and she guzzles gas;
I must admit, she's past her prime!

She is full of dents and scratches.
Her blue paint is cracked and peeling.
The carpet is torn, worn clear through.
The cloth has come off the ceiling.

She's old, but she's reliable.
Her motor, brakes, and trans work fine.
She gets me where I have to go,
And she is paid for! She's all mine!

(This poem was seond-place winner in the Monthly Contest of
McGroarty Chapter, California Federation of Chaparral Poets,
Inc., February 28, 2004).

To Ursula

Uncovering our unknown talents
Reaching into our hearts and souls,
Showing us how to express ourselves
Ultimately to reach our goals.
Lovingly you teach us all to be
Authors, connoisseurs of poetry.

Thank you for being part of our lives!

Get well soon! Good health again be yours!
Illness forever in your past!
Be gone, hernia and cataract!
Sunshiny days be yours at last!
Our wish: Rest, be stronger than before.
Now, teach your poetry class once more!

Music

Glorious music fills the air.
Joy abounds with every melody.
My heart and soul soar! It seems as if
The music was written just for me!

Grand opera is my passion!
Each note lingers in my memory.
Favorite composers: I'll name a few—
Mozart, Puccini, Bizet, Verdi.

Carmen is Bizet's most well-known work.
His *Pearlfishers* is sheer ecstasy!
Mozart's *Magic Flute*: political
Satire hidden in fantasy.

Bellini's *Norma*, Verdi's *Aida*,
Puccini's *Madama Butterfly;*
Beautiful notes tell of tragedy,
But happy endings would satisfy!

Music connects us to times gone by;
Sublime pleasure without compare!
As long as there are geniuses,
Music will joyfully fill the air!

(This poem won 2nd Place on May 23, 2004 in the McGroarty Chapter,
California Federation of Chapararal Poets, Inc., Monthly Contest.)

Neglected

Thursday was a very busy day.
Papers ready, our tax man was here.
Macy's for pans, Mervyn's for slippers.
Oh! to relax! Errands interfere.

Friday Hoffi's puppy shots were done,
Leash, collar, and chew bones for our boy.
Candles, wine and challah all in place;
Prayers said. Shabbat peace we did enjoy.

Saturday, Chaparral Poets met.
Sharing recent works was a delight.
Sunday a day of rest? Not for me!
Wash, letters, calls: busy, dawn to night.

Monday the house was cleaned, groceries bought.
Wash was finished, some deskwork was done.
I tackled the unanswered letters.
It seems that we write to everyone!

Tuesday was here before I knew it.
Little time to read or watch T.V.
Scrapbooks are still waiting to be done.
Time just seems to get away from me!

Hopefully, now you have an idea
What I did not do this week as planned.
Wednesday is class. Homework neglected.
I'll try harder— please understand!

My Muse

(Cinquain)

Suffering

from writer's block.

My pen lies idle, still.

I scold my Muse, beg, plead, cajole;

Success!

Upsetting Nature's Plan

(Senryu)

Spring: set clocks ahead.

Fall: Set them back once again.

Folly: Leave them be!

(Senryu)

Haiku poetry:

Just seventeen syllables;

Lovely word pictures.

Getting Older

(Senryu)

My mind makes long lists

Of all the things I must do;

My body says, "No!"

Sweet pansy faces

purple, yellow, pink and blue

Smile as I walk by.

The Assignment

The assignment for poetry class
Was to write a short poem that rhymed.
But no topic was given, alas;
My imagination must be primed!

Should I write about the stars and moon?
That subject has been so overdone!
Teacher chided, "Don't rhyme 'June, moon, spoon'."
I am stumped before I have begun!

My new pup has his very own rhyme.
I've written about my family.
I'll do politics some other time.
No subject seems to call out to me.

I write a line or two, then I pause.
I check my rhyming dictionary.
Time for this poem to end, because
I can't find words that fit perfectly.

No topic picked. I'm not defeated!
Twenty lines have been composed, you see.
The assignment has been completed.
I have written rhyming poetry!

Ode to a Great Man

Ronald Wilson Reagan
1911-2004

Death claimed Ronald Wilson Reagan today.
U.S. lost her Great Communicator.
The world will miss him more than words can say.
His deeds will be remembered evermore.
Simple beginnings, he rose to greatness.
Who expected as much from an actor?

California Governor—great success!
Consummate Patriot—he loved this country.
President—his energy was boundless;
As was his love for his dear wife, Nancy.
He made us proud to be American!
Communism, Berlin Wall fell. They were free!

'Tis the Long Goodbye to a gentle man.
Peace! We must continue work he began.

Memorial

To Dr. William M. Kramer:
June 14, 2004

Dear Rabbi Bill,

Young, we looked for a Temple family.
We saw you on the Louis Lomax show.
You welcomed us with open arms, did decree
"Rabbi means teacher. We'll share what we know."

Met Dad in the hospital, talked for hours.
Kindred souls: man of God and atheist!
"I see God and Jack having a discussion
To convince each other they do not exist!"

George's Bar Mitzvah; illness; you were there.
You called Germany to allay our fears.
Shabbat of Thanksgiving! Joy without compare!
Lori's wedding. You shared laughter and tears.

You were our treasured friend, teacher, Rabbi.
Always in our hearts! Too soon to say "goodbye".

    Love, Lynne G. Schwalbe.

(This poem won 2nd Place on 6-26-04, in the McGroarty Chapter,
California Federation of Chaparral Poets, Inc., Monthly Contest.)

Now and Then

The scale tells me a truth I simply cannot comprehend.
My mind automatically sees hundred pounds less than shown.
My girth and my weight I must significantly amend—
If I lose eighty pounds, I'll be back to the weight once known.

I've been told that I'm not too fat, just too short for my weight;
If I were seven feet four, I'd not own an extra pound!
Just once I'd like to hear Doctor say, then I'd celebrate:
"You need to gain ten pounds, Lynne, and your good health will
abound.

I provide warmth in the winter and shade in the summer—
But Max doesn't realize that his comfort I guarantee!
My grandchildren's comment when young caused a lot of laughter:
They said they love to hug me because I'm "soft and squishy!"

Can't believe I'm sixty-nine! How did years fly by so fast?
Mirror tells me I'm older; I'm still young in my mind's eye.
Upper arms wiggle. My future too quickly becomes my past.
Wrinkles, gray hair. Denial is my *modus operandi*!

I see the young woman of forty or fifty years ago
So full of life, hope, optimism, and a future bright.
Arthritis denies me pain-free freedom I used to know;
Running barefoot through grass, and more, I recall with delight.

I'm content with good health, and the love of my family.
My children and all my grandchildren mean the world to me!
My goal: to strive each day to be the best I can be;
To live life well, and pray to God I will age gracefully!

Why I Take the Saturday Poetry Class

Taught since I was five
To compose poetry,
With Dad's encouragement
I gained proficiency.

Throughout school days I wrote.
Then marriage, family
Took all my time and stopped
My creativity.

My Muse was ignored so
She stopped talking to me.
The years quickly flew by
With no new poetry.

Then, just last September,
the *Burbank Leader* said,
"Poetry classes starting."
I signed up, excited.

'Twas time again to write.
Slumber no more, my Muse!
Thrilled I attended class.
More knowledge I can use!

Ursula is a gem!
With humor we are taught
Meter, rhyme, free verse, and more.
Happiness she has brought!

Published throughout the world,
Her poems do delight.
They capture life's moments,
Say, "Things will be all right!"

Soon it was apparent
That eight weeks would not do.
We convinced our teacher
Classes must continue!

I'm writing more than ever!
May classes never end!
More than just a teacher,
She's mentor, and our friend.

Poetry

(an alphabet poem)

Always to be enjoyed.
Beautiful words by author employed.
Chosen to express a thought;
Delighting us just as they ought!
Excitement! Joy! Sadness, too.
Formal way to say, "Adieu".
Greetings of a diverse sort;
Helping hand offering comfort.
Impossible apology?
Just write, "Sorry. Forgive me."
Kisses, hugs, words of endearment;
Lovers hope, then acknowledgement!
Many times life can be absurd!
Naught says it like the written word.
Oh, how full our lives can be!
Perfect for heart and soul: POETRY!

The Washing Machine

(Villanelle)

The washing machine does not spin!
Bought a Maytag to have the best.
No matter what I do, I can't win!

Called insurance company, cryin'.
Dealing with them is quite a test.
The washing machine does not spin!

I called them again and again.
Wrote the C.E.O. I'm depressed.
No matter what I do, I can't win!

I need the magic of Merlin!
Trips to the laundromat I detest!
The washing machine does not spin!

Inept jerks put the wrong parts in,
So the Maytag man did attest.
No matter what I do, I can't win!

Insurance company did listen!
With a new washer I am blessed!
The washing machine does now spin!
It matters what I do! I can win!

What Stories I Could Tell!

Life began a hundred twenty years ago.
Oui! I am a fine French Mademoiselle.
I've had many wonderful adventures.
If I could talk, what stories I could tell!

My earliest years were spent in Europe.
Aristocrats, country folk treated me well.
Salt air, rolling waves, sickness: I crossed the sea.
If I could talk, what stories I could tell!

Ended up at a fancy antique store.
I was refurbished, and now I look swell.
'Twas lonely, waiting for the right family.
If I could talk, what stories I could tell!

My short, shapely legs are beautifully carved.
Termite holes adorn my backside, sad to tell.
Brass drawer handles and lock add patina, charm.
If I could talk, what stories I could tell!

There's a large dark spot in my center drawer,
From a leaking pen or spilled ink well.
But I think that just gives me character!
If I could talk, what stories I could tell!

My kneehole is far too small for comfort,
And my drawers stick quite often, truth to tell.
What do you expect from an old lady?
If I could talk, what stories I could tell!

In '92, I came home to Burbank.
I'm Lynne's French Provincial desk. I'm treated well.
This is my family; forever I'll stay.
If I could talk, what stories I could tell.

(An exercise in Imagery, Personification, and Echo)

Legacy

(Pantoum)

It's up to me to be the best that I can be!
Family traits make me who I am, it's true.
It's just a crapshoot; there's no guarantee.
Genes matter, but it depends on what I do!

Family traits make me who I am, it's true.
Intelligence, compassion, love beyond compare—
Genes matter, but it depends on what I do!
Mom and Dad had many good traits to share.

Intelligence, compassion, love beyond compare—
These are my wonderful, precious legacy.
Mom and Dad had many good traits to share!
Love of learning, optimism, honesty.

These are my wonderful, precious legacy.
But extra weight, and a temper I must defeat.
Love of learning, optimism, honesty;
Good health and my family make my life complete.

But extra weight, and a temper I must defeat.
It's just a crapshoot; there's no guarantee!
Good health and my family make my life complete.
It's up to me to be the best that I can be!

(This poem won 3rd Prize on Oct. 20, 2004 in the McGroarty
Chapter, California Federation of Chaparral Poets, Inc., Monthly
Contest.)

III

Expressions of Love

This photograph was created by Richard Williams
Photography, Glendale, CA in 1986.
Permission for use granted by Richard Williams, 3-18-2005

I Wonder

The ocean ebbs and flows as it did before I was born.

The sun and the moon take turns illuminating the Earth.

The rain, snow and sunshine come and go as the seasons pass

Just as they had always done before the day of my birth.

The flowers bloom. Birds fill the air with their glorious song.

I often ask, "Have I made a difference? Can I do more?"

Yes, of course I can! But I love, and I am loved,

So our world is a much better place than it was before.

Love Changed

Met on a blind date in 1953.
Walked the Golden Gate Bridge, my new love and I.
Meant for each other, we knew we would wed.
Fireworks! Just like on the Fourth of July!

Thanks to "Queen for a Day," we got a good start.
Honeymoon, washer, other gifts were won.
Carefree, and so much in love, we saw our years fly by;
Careers, saving for a house, and time for fun.
    Love changed.

Lori joined our family in nineteen fifty eight.
In nineteen sixty one, George was adopted.
Hectic life! Little time to nurture our love.
We knew each other's thoughts, though few words were said.

Through the good times and bad, our love remained strong.
Like a ship in safe harbor, we were secure.
In each other's arms, we felt safe from all harm.
Happy, we enjoyed the marriage adventure!

Our children grew up and went out on their own.
With empty nest a fact we could not ignore,
Had to learn about each other all over again,
For the youth we loved wasn't there any more!
    Love changed.

After forty-two years came the shock of my life.
Divorce! This couldn't be happening to us!
I felt alone, bereft, a ship lost at sea.
Anger and disappointment the impetus.

What did I see in him? How could I have loved him?
Then acceptance, independence came to me.
New adventures and new friends were mine at last.
I'm stronger than I ever thought I could be!
    Love changed.

Life has a funny way of surprising us.
Never thought it would be. Together once more,
Doubts have disappeared. Whatever lies ahead
Right for each other, it's better than before.

Physical limitations must be endured;
But the things I cannot do, he does for me.
And when he needs help getting up and such,
I help to the best of my ability.

Now our love is like an old pair of slippers;
Comfy, slightly worn, easy to step into.
Can't imagine life without Max by my side.
I know joy when he smiles and says, "I love you!"
    Love changed.

(This poem won 3rd prize, in the McGroarty Chapter, California
Federation of Chaparral Poets, Inc., Monthly Contest, —date not
recorded)

Our Miracle

*(in honor of Lisa and Gerald's 12th birthday,
February 22, 2002)*

Watching our daughter grow bigger with each passing day
Is the miracle of miracles! A long-awaited joy!
After three years of desperate yearning and fervent prayers
Our Lori-Love is pregnant with a girl and a boy!

Grandma-to-Be takes pictures week by week, anxious
To record each spurt of her growth for posterity,
Only to discover close to the blessed event
That film was forgotten, and the camera is empty!

After months of waiting, there's only two weeks to go,
But the little ones can't wait to meet their family.
So while our London cousins are sleeping, the call comes:
"If you want to see them born, come immediately!"

Excited and so happy, we rush to St. Joseph's.
We barely have time to kiss our girl and say, "Good luck!"
Then she's whisked to surgery, and before we know it,
The twins are born! We are ecstatic and awestruck.

Watching our grandchildren in their first moments of life
Is an indescribable Joy, and my heart sings!
We stand by the nursery window for over an hour
Dreaming of their future, and counting our blessings.

Moving

(Senryu sequence)

Love must be free to
soar with grace, take its own path;
and at last, find home.

Lori-Love. Great Joy!
Sweet daughter. God's greatest gift.
The light of our lives.

Even though my heart
is breaking, I let them go
to follow their dreams.

Freckles,

M.P.P., M.P.O.L.
a.k.a. Picadilly Miss Fancy Prance

A large box of squealing, squirming black-and-white balls of fur—
Ten six-week-old English Springer Spaniels— what a sight!
Very quickly, we fell in love with the **M**ost **P**recious **P**up.
For twelve years you have been our friend and a sheer delight.

Now, let's go back to the beginning of your life's story.
Our labrador, Shana, was alone. You joined our family.
Fourteen, she was glad to spend her days basking in the sun.
You were a hyper lass, full of endless energy.

We lost Shana when you were two. It was your turn to grieve.
Amanda Foundation introduced us to your new friend.
Bobbi, a year-old Brittany-Collie mix won our hearts.
You two were inseparable, your antics were legend.

Obedience classes were your forte. We won First Place.
Bobbi and Dad didn't do well, it was plain to see.
Assuming the right position you taught Bobbi to dig;
Then you stood by so proudly, watching your prodigy!

Waiting for peaches to ripen was a favorite pastime.
The two of you pushed the trunk and shook the laden tree.
Then as the peaches fell, you each took one between your paws
And lay there content, enjoying the sweet delicacy.

Bobby died quite suddenly when she was just nine years old.
You searched for her for weeks, but alas, you were alone.
An eager eater, now you needed to be coaxed and cajoled.
Bereft, you took some of her behavior for your own.

Wed for four decades, Max had new desires for his life.
Unexpectedly, he told me of his plans to go.
I lay in bed crying. You jumped up, snuggled by my side,
Kissed away my tears. Any wonder I love you so?

"Do you want a boney?" "Are you hungry?" "That's a good girl!"
Your loving glance shows you understand, are observant.
Sad when I go, you wag your tail to welcome me back home.
Most **P**recious **O**ld **L**ady— friend, companion, confidant.

Except for arthritis, you seemed to age quite gracefully.
Then in July, you fell on the floor and could not stand.
Stiff joints and pain plague us both and curb our activity.
We take Glucosamine Condroitin— same dose, same brand!

A physical revealed you have a liver problem, too.
Antibiotics were tried with hope you would be cured.
Next would be x-rays, biopsy, surgery. I agonized!
The vet counseled the pain and risk should not be endured.

I wonder, is our choice to just let Nature take its course—
For you to live your natural life, the right thing to do?
You are the best dog ever was, ever will be, dear girl.
We will cherish each day together and just LOVE YOU!

Veteran's Day, November 11, 2003

Max, dear, 50 years ago today, you proposed.

I cannot help but wonder why you choose this day.

Who could have possibly known, who would have supposed

That our lives together would have turned out this way?

We were so much in love that summer of '53;

With joy we planned our future as husband and wife

We thought our love would help us live in harmony,

But instead, most years were full of tension and strife.

After 42 years we went our separate ways.

We are a couple again, but we're not the same.

More mature, we get along much better these days,

For you see, we are veterans of the marriage game.

Yesterday Was Friday

Yesterday was Friday.
The day of days was here!
Hung the flag bright and early
To wish Max birthday cheer.

I straightened up the house.
Max picked up cake and food.
Lori and kids came at three,
All in a festive mood.

They left for a while.
Dental visits waited.
Last minute chores done knowing
All was appreciated.

The gathering was small.
Work, illness kept some away.
But Max felt love and happiness
On his very special day.

Yesterday was Friday.
Seventy-fifth Birthday!
Party is a memory.
May health and joy come your way!

Freckles

"Pic-a-dilly Miss Fancy Prance"
(May 1, 1991— January 2, 2004)

Dear Sweet Precious Girl,

Your valiant struggle is over.
You left us today.
Taking you to the vet
    was one of the most difficult things
we've ever had to do.
But it was time.
You were almost blind
    and kept bumping into walls and furniture.
You had little hearing left.
When you had an accident in the house,
    you looked at me with your beautiful black eyes full of shame,
    as if to say, "I'm sorry, Mom."

You could barely get up and down,
    and you slept most of the time.
The last two days, you could not eat.
Worst of all, the vet said that
    now you were in pain and were suffering.
Extreme medicines could have prolonged
    your life for three or four weeks;
    but you would not be comfortable.
        That's not living!

I see you and Bobbi
    playing and running free again.
Find my Dad;
    he will love you as much as we do.

You are the dearest, sweetest dog
    that ever was, ever will be.
Thank you for being
    our very special Lover-Girl.
We love you, and we miss you.
You will live in our hearts forever.
    Goodbye, dear friend.

Lover Boy

I did not want another dog pal
After our beloved Freckles died,
But Freckles had other plans for us
That simply would not be denied.

We visited shelters several times
To find a dog for our family.
They were too big, too small, too old.
We decided to wait patiently.

Then I asked Freckles to intercede.
"We loved you so! Help us! was my plea.
I know for sure she heard my prayer.
At Peggy Woods', 'twas love instantly.

A ten-week-old cocker spaniel pup
Was waiting. He's a beautiful boy!
Once in my arms, I knew he'd come home.
He's a lot of work, but fills our hearts with joy!

Soft as silk, he's a golden tan and white;
Big brown eyes; tail that wags constantly.
Opera lovers, for us his name was a breeze:
"Oftenbarks Tails of Hoffman"— "Hoffi!"

We were told to cage-train him; it's cruel
To keep him there twenty-four hours a day.
We tell him what to do; love him lots.
We're training him the old-fashioned way.

Hope his puppy bites and accidents
Will soon be a distant memory.
We'll work on digging when the time comes.
He will learn— he's smart as he can be!

We've had Hoffi three weeks, and he knows,
"Want to go outside?" "Go, good Boy!" and more.
"Are you hungry? Do you want to eat?"
He runs so fast he slides across the floor!

"Where's my Hoffi? Hoffi, come!" He's here.
Sits by the counter, barks for his boney.
Pillows provided for his comfort
Are ignored to sleep in bed with me!

May we enjoy happy, healthy years
With our darling, lovable Hoffi.
Is he spoiled? Oh, just a little bit!
No doubt he rules our home completely!

Hoffi

Hoffi is our cocker spaniel pup.
He's sweet and loveable as can be.
He sleeps on his back, legs wide apart,
So his jewels are there for all to see!

We could get him some trousers to wear,
But we decided to let him be.
He's the perfect dog—nothing's lacking
Except that he has no modesty!

Argument

We had another argument.
I can't even remember why.
Work? Children? Money? T.V. Sports?
Without meaning to, tempers fly.

It's hard to admit, "I was wrong."
We're both strong-willed and want our way.
If, instead of yelling, we'd whisper,
"I love you," peace would rule the day.

The sunrise of each brand new day
Brings a chance to set things right.
A kiss, a hug, a smile all tell,
"I love you, morning, noon, and night."

(This poem was first-place winner in the Monthly Contest
McGroarty Chapter, California Federation of Chaparral Poets, Inc.
on 12-27-03, and was Second Place Annual Winner there for 2003.)

Three Little Words

(Tanka)

"I love you!"

He told her one fine day.

"I love you!"

She shyly replied.

Married for fifty years!

Golden Anniversary

(Italian Sonnet)

It's been fifty years since our vows were said.
"Love, honor, cherish 'til Death do us part."
Our love has stayed strong through the years, Sweetheart,
Though many events were unintended.

Years have flown by since we were newly-wed.
We've had many challenges from the start.
Health, loss, divorce could have torn us apart.
You are my strength, my joy, my Beloved.

After years apart, we're together now.
Differences resolved and arguments done,
Our new, much happier life has begun.
To live in harmony, our solemn vow!

In spite of wrongs we have done and been through
We are soulmates for life, and I love you!

Melina Marie

(For August 6, 2004)

Happy Birthday, Melina Marie!
You are just as sweet as you can be!
Since you were born, years have flown away.
You're growing so fast! You're six today!

You are a good friend and do well in school;
Mind your parents, follow the Golden Rule.
Your loving nature thrilled us from the start.
Do your best, and follow your dreams, Sweetheart.

Great Grandma and Great Grandpa love you so!
We're proud of you, and just want you to know
We wish you days filled with Joy and Laughter;
Health and Happiness forever after!

Love, Grandma Lynne and Grandpa Max.

Congratulations!

(Triolet)

Dear Lori:

We're so very proud of you.
As a daughter, you're the best!
You excel in all you do.
We're so very proud of you!
Now your studying is through—
You passed the Real Estate test!
We're so very proud of you!
As a daughter, you're the best!

Love, Mom and Dad

Counting

"1-2-3-4-5-6-7-8.
Grandma, we're going to be late!"
Lisa and Gerald, barely three,
Are playing the signal game with me.

"Red light, red light!" they shout with glee
And start to count immediately.
"This is a long one, up to 35!
It's green now, Grandma. You can drive!"

Another signal appears ahead.
"Grandma, Grandma, it's turning red!"
They start to count, "1-2-3.
How long do you think this one will be?"

Invented to keep them occupied,
Sitting in the back seat, side by side,
They think the game is lots of fun;
Know colors and counting when they're done.

They played this game for years with me.
Now they're 15, it's a favorite memory.

What Love Means

Love means missing that special someone when they're away;
Love means not letting the little things get in the way.
Love means loving your partner unconditionally.
Love means knowing and sharing trust and fidelity.

Love means that a touch, a hug, and a kiss make you thrill.
After all these years, a smile gives you shivers, still.
Appreciating qualities you liked when you met,
And ignoring the habits you would like to forget!

Love means working at your marriage each day,
Understanding and compromise go such a long way!
Having patience and courage when the going gets tough;
Love means counting your blessings and knowing they're enough.

Love means ignoring wrinkles, baldness, and increased size;
In other words, seeing each other through lovers' eyes.
Happy to be together for the rest of your days,
Saying, "I love you today, tomorrow, and always."

Because

I love you because
    your smile lights up a room and
    after all these years stills sets my heart a-flutter.
I love you because
    you are patient and slow to anger,
    and you never hold a grudge— for long!
I love you because
    you see the good in people
    and always try to make the best of any situation.
I love you because
    you have always worked hard
    to provide for our family.
I love you because
    in spite of your rigid German upbringing
    you try to be flexible.
I love you because
    you do your best to get me out of
    the silly situations I get myself into!
I love you because
    your gentle nature calms my explosive nature
    and restores peace and harmony to our home.
I love you because
    you share and encourage my hopes and dreams
    and you want me to be the best I can be.
I love you because
    you love me.

(This poem won 3rd Prize in the McGroarty Chapter, California
Federation of Chaparral Poets, Inc., Monthly Contest, March 26,
2005).

A Smile Gives You Shivers, Still

An Alphabetical Index of Poems

Printed in the United States
41040LVS00007B/4-12